POISONOUS SNAKES

POISONOUS SNAKES

GEORGE S. FICHTER

FRANKLIN WATTS
NEW YORK | LONDON | TORONTO | SYDNEY | 1982
A FIRST BOOK

Cover photograph courtesy of Bruce Colman, Inc.

Photographs courtesy of: The American Museum of Natural History: pp. opposite 1, 3, 8, 13, 24, 38, 53, 57; Culver Pictures: p. 14; New York Zoological Society: pp. 19, 22, 25, 41, 49; Photo Researchers: pp. 32, 48 (McHugh); U.S. Sport Fisheries & Wildlife: pp. 42 (Haddon), 45 (Piper); Bruce Coleman (E.R. Degginger): p. 60.

Library of Congress Cataloging in Publication Data

Fichter, George S.
  Poisonous snakes.

  (A First book)
  Bibliography: p.
  Includes index.
  Summary: Discusses the best known of the poisonous snakes, which use poison mainly for killing or paralyzing their prey, as an aid to digestion, and for protection.
  1. Poisonous snakes—Juvenile literature. [1. Poisonous snakes. 2. Snakes] I. Title.
QL666.06F367   597.96′0469   81-16242
ISBN 0-531-04349-5   AACR2

CONTENTS

Mexican moccasins

(1) POISONOUS SNAKES

Of all the animals in the world, snakes rank among the most misunderstood and feared. Much of the fear is based on superstition. Centuries-old myths about snakes still persist. Typical tales picture these silent, legless creatures as "evil" and "slimy." Neither is true. Few have bad tempers, and snakeskin is dry and scaly or satiny rather than slimy. Not many snakes are poisonous—only about 300 of the 2,500 to 3,000 species in the world.

All snakes, including those that are poisonous, are predators—that is they hunt and eat other animals. They play an important and valuable role in nature. Many make their meals exclusively of such "pest animals" as rats and mice.

This book is about the best known of the poisonous snakes. Their venom, or poison, serves mainly for killing or paralyzing their prey. It is an aid to digestion, as well, and it may also be used for protection. Very few snakes, either poisonous or harmless, are aggressive. Finding themselves in danger, they try first to escape, although they will bite if they are cornered.

Most bites from poisonous snakes are accidental; some are due to foolish or careless handling. An estimated world total of 35,000 to 40,000 people die from snakebite every year. Most of these deaths—about 30,000—occur in Southeast Asia. Poisonous snakes are abundant there, and much of the population goes about with bare feet and legs. In addition, proper medical treatment is often neglected or not available. Those snakes taking the highest toll are Russell's viper and the Asiatic cobra. In North America about 6,000 people are bitten by poisonous snakes every year, but very few die. Estimates vary from an average of 15 to as few as 2. With proper medical attention these deaths could also be avoided. By comparison more than 1,000 people in the United State die every year from the stings of bees and wasps.

IDENTIFYING POISONOUS SNAKES

No single feature distinguishes all poisonous snakes. A broad triangular head? The dangerous vipers do have a wide, wedge-shaped head, broad at the back of the jaws where the large poison glands are located. But some harmless snakes also have triangular heads while many of the most dangerous snakes do not. The beautiful coral snakes and their relatives, for example, have a slim head, as do most harmless species.

THE FAMILIES OF POISONOUS SNAKES

Poisonous snakes belong to one of the following groups.

Hog-nosed viper (left); Godman's viper (right).

The elapids (family Elapidae) are most abundant in Asia, Africa, and Australia. (In Australia they are the sole family of poisonous snakes.) There are also some elapids in North and South America. This is the family to which cobras, kraits, and coral snakes belong. Most are slender. They have short, stationary or fixed fangs at the front of the upper jaw.

Closely related to the elapids are the sea snakes (family Hydrophidae. Most of them live in the warm tropical Pacific and Indian Oceans off Australia and southern Asia. All sea snakes have very poisonous venom. They are not particularly dangerous to humans, however, because they are slow to bite and have very small mouths. Like elapids they have fixed front fangs. The sides and tail of most sea snakes are greatly flattened from side to side which suits them for life in the water, but makes it difficult for them to move on land.

The vipers (family Viperidae) have a well-developed mechanism for injecting venom. Their large front fangs are not fixed but hinged and folded against the roof of the mouth when not in use. The fangs are hollow with a canal through which the venom is injected. Compared to most snakes, vipers are thick-bodied.

Vipers may be divided into two important subfamilies: true, or Old World, vipers, and pit vipers. True vipers live in Europe, Asia, and Africa. There are none in the New World.

Pit vipers, sometimes given separate family rank, resemble the true vipers. But they are distinguished by a deep depression or "pit" between the eye and the nostril on each side of the head. This organ is sensitive to heat, and is used to detect warm-blooded prey. Rattlesnakes, copperheads, and cottonmouths, or water moccasins, are members of this family.

Finally, there are the colubrids, only two of which are highly poisonous. Snakes of the family Colubridae are found throughout the world wherever snakes exist. This is the largest family of snakes, and nearly all the roughly 2,000 species are harmless. Racers, garter snakes, king snakes, and most other common and familiar snakes belong to this family. In southern Africa, however, two of the colubrid snakes are truly venomous. They are the boomslang and the bird snake. Their venom, particularly that of the boomslang, is very powerful. Unlike other poisonous snakes they are "rear-fanged." Their fangs are at the back of the upper jaw.

Some other colubrid snakes may have mildly toxic saliva that slows down or even paralyzes their prey. But their bite is not dangerous to humans. It can be treated with the same antiseptic that would be used on a cut or scratch.

(2)
VENOMS

A snake's venom is produced by enlarged, specialized salivary glands. Its primary use is for killing or paralyzing the live animals on which the snake feeds. But the venoms of most poisonous snakes are far more potent than necessary for killing their prey. A big king cobra, for example, eats snakes its own size or smaller, but it has enough powerful poison to kill several elephants. It is this extravagance in amount and potency that makes venomous snakes dangerous to humans.

Poisonous snakes inject the venom into bite wounds through their fangs. These teeth are hollow in some species and grooved in others. They connect directly to ducts, or tubes, leading to the poison glands. The teeth thus operate much like hypodermic needles. In true vipers and pit vipers, the fangs are so large the snake cannot close its mouth when they are extended, ready to bite. But the fangs can be folded back so they fit against the roof of the mouth. When the mouth opens to bite, the fangs spring forward. The fangs of vipers are located at the front of the mouth as are the small fangs of elapids and sea snakes. But the fangs of the few poisonous colubrid snakes are at the rear of the upper jaw and have only a gutterlike groove down which the venom runs into the bite wound.

Interestingly, a poisonous snake may bite without injecting venom. Furthermore, the snake can release its venom through both fangs at the same time or from only the right or the left fang. The snake may also inject all the venom in its glands with a single bite or only a little of the venom at a time. The amount of venom delivered appears related to the kind and size of prey. It also appears to increase when the snake is excited or irritated. Knowing this, snake handlers may tease their snakes to get the maximum amount of venom from them.

Snake venoms are complex proteins. At one time they were divided into two simple categories: those affecting the nervous system (neurotoxins) and those affecting the circulatory system (hemotoxins). Now we know that most venoms are mixtures or blends of both types, with one of the two dominating.

The venom of the rattlesnakes of North America is mostly hemotoxic. There is immediate pain, swelling, and change of skin color in the area of the bite as blood vessels and surrounding tissues are destroyed. Because of the puncture or holes made by the large fangs, the bite is generally easy to see.

Coral snake venom, like the venoms of cobras and other elapids, is primarily neurotoxic. The bite is usually painful—like a sting—but there is little effect on the tissues in the immediate area of the bite. Because these snakes have small fangs, the puncture marks where the venom was injected may be difficult to find. The danger from venoms of this sort comes later when the poison has traveled to critical

nerve centers that control breathing and heartbeat. If death occurs, it is almost always from breathing paralysis. The delayed reaction is one of the most important reasons why snakebite victims must be taken to a hospital as soon as possible. There they can be treated with antivenin, which counteracts the poison. At a hospital, too, artificial breathing devices are at hand to help a bite victim whose ability to breathe suddenly fails.

VENOM EXTRACTION

The venoms of many kinds of snakes are used in medical research and to lessen the pain of some kinds of illnesses. They are also used to produce serum, or antivenin, for treating snakebites.

Professional snake handlers extract the venom from snakes collected in the wild or raised in captivity for just this purpose. To get the venom, each snake must be handled. In one method, its fangs are made to puncture a thin cover stretched tightly over a sterile glass container. The venom released by the snake collects in the bottom of the container.

Another, less satisfactory method is to let the snake bite a rubber ball or some similar object from which the venom can be removed. This method is more likely to be used with back-fanged snakes. Handling the snake is dangerous, but it is the best way to get the most venom possible. If the snake were allowed to strike and release its venom at random, most would be lost.

"Milking" a rattlesnake.

Any method of collecting venom may be referred to as "milking" the snake. Strictly speaking, however, milking consists of squeezing the venom from the snake's glands. This can damage the glands and limit the snake's ability to produce more venom. If it is done often, it can even kill the snake. Many experts today extract only as much venom as the snake ejects spontaneously in the act of biting. As a result hundreds of extractions may be taken from the same snake if it is well cared for in captivity. A pampered 14-foot (4.3-m) king cobra, for example, may yield as much as 610 mg, or about 120 drops, or venom at a time and may continue to produce venom for many years.

The main use for venoms is in making antivenins for treating snakebite. These are made by injecting venom into a horse starting with a small dose and increasing the dose until the horse has built up an immunity to the poison. Then some of the blood from the horse is treated to make antivenin. A person who has been bitten by a snake receives the kind of antivenin that will counteract the poison. An antivenin that can be used for the bite of a coral snake would not be useful in treating the bite of a rattlesnake which has an entirely different kind of venom. For this reason it is important to know, if possible, what kind of snake delivered the bite.

Other medical uses for venom have been tried in the past. Venoms have been used without much success in treating cases of leprosy, epilepsy, and some eye diseases. But new medical uses of venoms that look promising are being developed. Some kinds of venoms, for example, are useful because they contain elements (called anticoagulants) that prevent the clotting of blood. Ordinarily, blood clotting is nature's protection against excess loss of blood from wounds. But sometimes blood clots can cause serious problems. Heart failure is sometimes due to a blood clot, or thrombus, that blocks the supply of blood to the heart. Clotting may also be a hazard in organ transplants. An anticoagulant can break up clots or prevent such clotting. The venom of the Malay pit viper, for example, is of special interest to medical researchers because it is not highly toxic but prevents clotting temporarily. The venom can be used almost "whole"—that is, without complicated processing.

Other venoms, such as those from cobras, may give relief from the severe pain of arthritis or cancer. In experimental cases patients given venom treatments have lost much of their anxiety and depression. Their spirits lift and they feel more cheerful. For this reason doctors are also looking into the possibility of using venom injections as treatment for some mental patients.

Venom may be useful in different kinds of pure research. Biochemists, for example, use venoms, or particular portions of them, to break up parts of cells into even smaller units that can in turn be investigated.

(3)
THE
COBRA
CLAN

The king cobra, probably the best known of all the poisonous snakes, is the giant of its clan and also the largest poisonous snake in the world. Most of these elapid snakes are about 10 feet (3m) long, but one is known to have exceeded 18 feet (5.5 m).

The king cobra lives mainly in the hilly jungle country of southeastern Asia. A few inhabit the Philippines and nearby islands. The king cobra makes its meals chiefly of other snakes and, unlike other cobras, usually hunts during the day. The cobra is the only snake known to build a true nest. The female makes her nest of leaves and grass. She uses loops of her body to push the material into a pile. When the nest is finished, it consists of two chambers. She lays her eggs in the lower chamber and occupies the upper chamber herself. She may come forth angrily to drive away intruders.

Much more common than the king cobra is the smaller Asiatic or Asian cobra, which averages 4 to 5 feet (1.2 to 1.5 m). Unlike the king cobra the Asiatic cobra hunts at night and eats mostly rats and mice. Searching for these rodents,

King cobra.

it often goes into houses and other buildings where it may come in contact with people.

In this part of the world, where much of the population walks barefooted and barelegged, the Asiatic cobra often stretches out on warm dirt trails. If it is stepped on by a person walking along the path, the snake reacts defensively by biting. Or a snake may be tucked into a pile of wood, waiting in ambush for rodents that are found in these places. A hand or a foot that comes too close may be struck by the alert, hunting reptiles. A snake may even find a blanket an ideal place to coil up for a rest. Occasionally someone going to bed finds out that a cobra has got there first and is not a willing snuggler. Partly because of frequent contact with people, the Asiatic cobra is responsible for roughly 75 percent of all the deaths in the world due to snakebites.

Like the king and other cobras, the Asiatic cobra spreads its hood when disturbed. It does this by lifting the extra-long ribs just behind the head and stretching the loose folds of skin that cover them, inflating this space with air. The thin, spread hood may be several times wider than the snake's body.

One race of the Asiatic cobra called the Indian cobra has a hood with "eyeglass" or "spectacle" marks on its back. An ancient myth traces the origin of these marks to Buddha. As the story is told, Buddha fell asleep after a day's travel. He would have been wakened by the sun shining in his eyes

**A snake charmer
with an Indian cobra.**

(15)

except for a kindly cobra that spread its hood to shield his eyes from the brightness. When Budda awoke he blessed the thoughtful snake and put his fingers against its hood, leaving the marks we see to this day.

The Asiatic cobra is the cobra commonly used by Indian snake charmers. They lift the lid of a basket in which a cobra is kept. Then, playing an instrument somewhat like a flute, they thrill their spectators by swaying back and forth in front of the snake as it rises majestically from the basket with its hood spread. The snake also moves back and forth rhythmically, following the movements of the performer. (Like all snakes, the cobra is deaf and cannot hear the music. But the music is an important part of the show.)

Sometimes the snake will strike. Snake charmers are skilled at their art, and they know the striking distance of the snake, but they do sometimes make mistakes. Some snake charmers remove the dangerous fangs to make the snakes harmless. Others sew the snake's mouth shut. These snakes do not live long, of course, for they rely on their fangs and venom to kill their prey.

Other snake charmers rely on the fact that these snakes are night hunters and, like owls, cannot see well enough during the day to strike with accuracy. Members of religious snake cults are unlikely to harm the reptiles, and their handling of snakes is skillful and dangerous.

AFRICAN COBRAS

Africa has more species of cobras than does Asia. All of the African cobras have small hoods. The most famous is the Egyptian cobra sometimes called an asp. This is probably the snake that the Egyptian Queen Cleopatra used to commit suicide. The Egyptian cobra averages 5 feet (1.5 m) in length but is known to reach 8 feet (2.4 m). Except for the rain forest and the sterile central desert, it ranges over much of Africa. It lives in all kinds of habitats from farmers' fields to brushy country to rocky hillsides. Over this wide area the snake varies considerably in color and pattern.

Reports are common that the Egyptian cobra is aggressive, but few of these tales are true. Like most snakes, it is really rather timid, but it will defend itself if it is cornered.

Two kinds of water cobras live in Africa in the Congo and eastern lake regions. These fish-eating snakes are always found near lakes, rivers, or streams. They average more than 5 feet (1.5 m) in length and occasionally reach 8 feet (2.4 m) or more. They are not aggressive, but they will bite in self defense. In typical cobra fashion, a water cobra lifts the front of its body off the ground and spreads its narrow hood as a warning when it is disturbed or molested.

Another African hood-spreading cobra is the Cape cobra. This slim reddish or yellowish 5- to 7-foot (1.5–2.1 m) snake lives in southern Africa. It does not look for trouble, but if approached, it raises its body and spreads its hood, prepared to strike. Its venom ranks among the most highly toxic.

One of the most dangerous of the African cobras is the spitting (or black-necked) cobra of tropical Africa. It inhabits the savannahs as well as fields cleared for farming or for livestock. This 6-foot (1.8 m) snake can actually "spit" or squirt its venom accurately at distances of about 8 feet (2.4 m). It aims for its victim's eyes. If the venom hits the eyes and is not flushed out immediately, it may cause temporary blindness. The spitting cobra varies in color. In some areas it is black all over; in others it may be pinkish tan.

Living in the same general region is the ringhal, which

can also "spit" its venom—squirting it from a small opening at the front of each of its two short fangs. Like the spitting cobra, it is "hair-triggered," needing little encouragement to eject its venom. Both the ringhal and the spitting cobra shoot their poison at an upward angle from each fang in a tiny, forceful stream. This breaks up quickly into a mistlike spray, but the snake is accurate at hitting its target from a distance of 6 feet (1.8 m) or more.

The ringhal's scales are strongly keeled: that is, a prominent ridge runs down the center of each scale. When the ringhal's hood is spread, it displays its black throat with one or two light bands near the base. Its back is dark brown with lighter brown crossbands. The ringhal averages less than 4 feet (1.2 m) in length.

MAMBAS OF AFRICA

African mambas are also elapids—that is, members of the same family as the cobras. Mambas are greatly feared, for these slim snakes have venom that is extremely dangerous —and they are large, alert, and very, very swift. They move about twice as fast as a person can walk. On the move a mamba is an awesome sight, gliding swiftly with its head and front third of its body off the ground.

There are many exaggerated stories of the ferocity of mambas. One tale describes the plight of a farmer who was plowing his field with a team of oxen when he accidentally

Eastern green mamba.

cut through a mamba's breeding ground. As the story goes, the infuriated snake gave quick and silent chase, first biting the man and then each of the oxen. Having taken its revenge, the snake returned to its disrupted lair.

Experts, today, agree that mambas are not particularly aggressive and use their amazing speed mainly to escape encounters with human beings. It seems true, however, that these excitable snakes do have a strong instinct for defending their territory, especially during the mating season.

When the mamba does strike, its speed makes it very impressive. As it moves forward, the snake hisses and flattens its neck. To strike, it propels as much as 40 percent of its body forward—about twice as much as other snakes. Compared to cobras and other elapids a mamba has long fangs, and they are located right up under the snout. The fangs are used in hunting birds, its principal prey, but the snake also eats rodents, which sometimes takes it into human dwellings. Despite their terrible reputation, bolstered by fiction and folklore, mambas do not rate high on the list of killers since they are rare in populated areas.

Black mambas live on the ground, but green mambas are arboreal, moving with agility through bushes and trees. The body of the snake stiffens to span the open spaces between branches. Four species of mambas inhabit Africa. All are slim for their length. Largest is the black mamba, which averages less than 10 feet (3 m) but may reach a length of 14 feet (4.3 m). The others are 6 to 7 feet (1.8 to 2.1 m) in length.

The black mamba is dark brown or gray. Its mouth has a bluish gray to black lining. All mambas, including the black, are green when young. Green mambas, however, are bright green as adults, an excellent camouflage in the foliage where they live. The inside of the green mamba's mouth is whitish blue. The scales of the west African green mamba, confined to the tropical rain forests of western Africa, are green edged with black. Jameson's mamba is two-toned. It has black-edged green scales in the front becoming darker and grading into totally black on the tail.

KRAITS OF SOUTHEAST ASIA

Kraits, close relatives of cobras, are abundant in southeastern Asia. A dozen species of these shiny, smooth-scaled and hoodless snakes are known. Most of them are handsome snakes. The banded krait, for example, has dark bands alternating with yellow or cream. These kraits may reach a length of 7 feet (2.1 m), but most are less than 5 feet (1.5 m) long. The Indian, Ceylon, Malayan, and many-banded kraits are also attractively banded. The redheaded krait has a bright red head and a black body with a bluish stripe down each side. Some also have an orange stripe down the middle of the body. Others are solid brown, black, or gray.

Kraits are sluggish during the day, but at night they become alert and active. Their diet consists mainly of other snakes, but they may also eat rats, mice, or any other easily available small animals. Kraits are not normally aggressive, but because they are plentiful and their hunting takes them near and into buildings, kraits come into contact with people regularly. The first reaction of most kraits is to coil and tuck their head out of sight under their body. But if stepped on or teased, they bite to protect themselves. The venom of most kraits is highly toxic.

Strange as it may seem, people living in these areas do not always realize—until they are bitten—how poisonous these mild-tempered snakes really are. Yet drop for drop, the venom of some kraits is more potent than that of the much-feared Asiatic cobra.

THE COLORFUL
CORAL SNAKES

Coral snakes are beautiful members of the cobra family. Like other elapids they have venom that affects mainly the nervous system, causing paralysis.

In the United States coral snakes live in the Southwest and in low coastal areas in the Southeast. They are slim and graceful, the head and body flowing together smoothly with no distinct neck. The small western coral snake averages about 1½ feet (.5 m) in length. The larger eastern species is 2 to 3½ feet (.6 to 1.1 m) long. In both, the snout is black as far back as the eye. This black snout is followed by alternating bands of yellow, black, yellow, and bright red that completely encircle the body. The broad black and red bands are always separated by narrower yellow bands. A common warning is "red against yellow kills a fellow." The harmless scarlet king snake that mimics the coral snake has a somewhat similar color pattern. But its snout is red, and the red and yellow bands are separated by narrower black bands. In the king snake the red is not next to the yellow band.

Coral snakes are generally docile. At first, most try to

**A banded krait from
the Malay Peninsula.**

(23)

In the coral snake (above), black and red
bands are separated by narrower yellow bands.
The nonpoisonous scarlet king snake (right)
imitates the colors of the coral snake,
but its red and yellow bands
are separated by black bands.

escape or to hide from danger. If getting away immediately is not easy, the snake usually tucks its head under a loop of its body and then lifts the tip of its tail and wiggles it. This may trick an attacker into watching the tail instead of the snake's dangerous head. Now and then an individual snake is really aggressive and quick to attack.

Coral snakes do not strike. They simply grab hold and begin chewing. Biting is difficult for coral snakes because they have a small mouth and tiny teeth less than ¼″ (.6 cm) long. The small, hollow fangs make only pinprick punctures in the skin, and the bite feels a little like a bee sting. The first effect is deceptive, however, for the venom reaches the breathing mechanism an hour or more later. Suddenly the victim cannot breathe. The diaphragm is paralyzed by the poison. For this reason it is very important to take a person bitten by a coral snake to a hospital as soon as possible. People find it difficult to believe that these small and beautiful snakes have such lethal poison, especially since the venom has only mild effects at first. Fortunately, deaths from coral snake bites in the United States are extremely rare—only about one every ten years.

More than three dozen other species of coral snakes live in Central and South America. Nearly all are similarly banded with black, yellow, and red. A Central American name for them, in fact, is *gargantilla*, which means "necklace." In some the yellow is replaced by cream or white, and two species are completely black. In others the rings do not go all the way around the body as they do in the species living in the United States. Some of the South American species are also large, reaching a length of more than 4 feet (1.2 m).

Nearly all coral snakes make their meals mainly of other snakes, but they will not refuse other small animals that are easily caught.

AUSTRALIA'S POISONOUS SNAKES

About 60 percent of all the species of snakes in Australia are poisonous, a distinction shared with no other continent. All of Australia's poisonous snakes are elapids—members of the same family as cobras. They sometimes flatten their bodies, but none has a well-developed hood. The venom of the majority is mild. Of the some seventy species of poisonous snakes in Australia, only a dozen or so are seriously dangerous to humans.

The giant among Australian poisonous snakes is the taipan, a dark coppery brown snake with a yellow belly commonly speckled with orange spots. It is known to attain a length of more than 10 feet (3 m), but few are more than 7 feet (2.1 m). Compared to other snakes in this family, the taipan's two curved fangs are very long. A seven-foot snake may have fangs more than half an inch (1.3 cm long).

When disturbed, the taipan flattens the front of its body and lifts it off the ground. Then it lashes its tail back and forth. This snake is easily irritated and quickly becomes aggressive. It strikes rapidly and repeatedly, then grabs hold firmly and chews as it injects large amounts of potent venom. Fortunately the taipan is not common. It is found only in northeastern Australia and New Guinea. Most authorities rank it as the most dangerous land snake in the world, and few if any people who are bitten survive.

In southern Australia the tiger snake is the most dangerous. Like the taipan it has extremely toxic venom. The tiger snake causes more deaths than the taipan because it is more abundant and lives in areas of greater population. Because the tiger snake hunts at night, most bites occur when the snake is accidentally stepped on. The snake re-

(27)

sponds quickly and defensively by biting. The venom is a quick-acting nerve poison that paralyzes breathing.

Tiger snakes 4 to 5 feet (1.2 to 1.5 m) are common, and occasionally there are reports of snakes 6 feet (1.8 m) or longer. The tiger snake is brownish or olive above, with dark tigerlike stripes or bands over a cream or white belly. Instead of laying eggs, the females give birth to their young—usually thirty or fewer but sometimes as many as a hundred at a time.

The fairly common Australian brown snake lives in the sandy soils and fields over most of Australia and also on the island of New Guinea. Averaging 5 to 6 feet (1.5 to 1.8 m) long, this swift snake is usually reddish brown with a lighter, yellowish-splotched belly. It is a nervous snake, easily irritated, and it takes an almost cobralike posture before striking. It flattens its neck slightly, holding it in an S-shaped loop. Although its venom is less potent than that of either the taipan or the tiger snake, the Australian brown snake is so widespread that is causes more deaths.

Unlike its many close relatives in Australia the brown snake lays twenty to thirty eggs instead of giving birth to young. The young snakes have a dark collar and three dozen or more crossbands.

The Australian black snake, about 5 to 6 feet (1.5 to 1.8 m) long, is glossy black above and reddish orange on the belly with crimson scales along the sides. It lives in swamps and damp forests along the coasts. This common snake is probably the best known of all Australia's poisonous snakes. It is shy, preferring to escape rather than to fight, but if cornered, it responds in the same way as other members of the elapid family—lifting the front of the body off the ground and flattening it by spreading the ribs. It first makes only mock strikes, but if pressed it will bite. The black snake is also well known for territorial duels in which two male snakes spar. They wrap their bodies around each other and roll over and over on the ground, hissing and "growling" noisily.

Because of its name the death adder might seem to be Australia's most fearsome snake. It is indeed highly poisonous, but drop for drop its venom is much less potent than that of the taipan or the tiger snake. It is powerful enough to kill a person, however, and that is what counts to someone who is bitten.

Adder is a name generally used for members of the viper family, but the Australian death adder belongs to the same family as cobras. Compared to these close relatives, however, it does have an unusually thick body, broad head, and short tail. These are definitely viperlike features. A few death adders measure more than 3 feet (.9 m) long, but most are 2 feet (.6 m) long. Found over most of the continent, the death adder becomes active at dusk and stays in hiding during the day often half buried in sand or loose soil. It cannot move rapidly, and so if it is disturbed, it defends itself by biting immediately.

The snakes described here are only the most common and most poisonous of those living in Australia and nearby. Remember that two out of three kinds of snakes in Australia are venomous and that more than half a dozen sea snakes inhabit Australia's waters, all of them poisonous. In fact, a snake encountered in Australia is more likely than not to be poisonous.

(4) SNAKES OF THE SEA

Sea snakes are the most abundant of all poisonous snakes. In all, there are about fifty species. They have small, fixed front fangs, like the members of the cobra clan. But because they have other distinctive features and habits, sea snakes are classified in a separate family.

At times off the coasts of Australia and southern Asia the surface of the sea seems alive with vast, writhing masses of these snakes in numbers so great they cannot be counted. Sometimes these incredible swarms consist of millions of snakes and extend over many miles. For most of the year, however, sea snakes are seen only occasionally, a few out at sea but most closer to shore, for sea snakes dislike the open ocean.

The venom of some species of sea snakes is many times more toxic than cobra venom. However, sea snakes cause very few deaths. One reason is that they are quite docile, even reluctant to bite. A sea snake is much more anxious to escape than it is to be aggressive, even when it is handled. When it does bite, it sometimes holds back its venom. Because of its very small mouth and tiny fangs, the sea snake also has trouble getting its teeth into a victim's flesh. Sea snakes are often caught in the nets of commercial fishermen who pick them out and toss them back into the sea as though they were strands of seaweed. Hook-and-line fishermen catch them, too. At times the snakes seem to be very inquisitive about swimmers and divers. They come close to stare, and they may even coil around a swimmer's arm or leg without attempting to bite.

Like whales and porpoises sea snakes are descended from ancestors that were land dwellers. In adapting to their marine environment, most of the sea snakes have acquired a large, oarlike tail flattened from side to side. The body is also flattened vertically. These adaptations enable them to swim powerfully through the sea. Some look very much like eels.

Because its nostrils open at the top of the snout, a sea snake can take in air at the surface without lifting its head out of the water. When it goes underwater, valves close to keep the water out of the nostrils. A greatly enlarged lung extends from the front of the body to the tail. This allows sea snakes to take in extraordinary amounts of air—enough to remain submerged for an hour or longer. Sea snakes have been seen at depths of 300 feet (91.4 m)!

Sea snakes have become so completely aquatic that they have difficulty moving on land. They have lost the broad, flat belly scales typical of land snakes and are almost as helpless on land as fish are out of water. However, some kinds do spend most of their lives in the mangroves along the shore and are out of the water as much as they are in it. A few kinds stray into fresh waters, and two species live in lakes. On land, sea snakes can bite, but they are not able to coil and strike as land snakes do.

As a group the sea snakes are mainly fish eaters. Some specialize in eating only fish eggs. Strange as it may seem the flesh of sea snakes is generally avoided by predator fish. Even if a sea snake is chopped up and offered in pieces, fish from the same natural habitat refuse to make a meal of them.

Most sea snakes are ovoviviparous—that is, the eggs are held in the female's body until they hatch. The female then gives birth to her young. In some species these newborn snakes are sizable—up to half as long as their mother. A few species lay eggs. One of these is the yellow-lipped sea krait that spends most of its time out of water and is the least well adapted for a totally aquatic life.

Four feet (1.2 m) is the average length of sea snakes. Longest is the colorful yellow sea snake, known to reach a length of 10 feet (3 m).

The yellow-bellied or black-and-yellow sea snake (the common sea snake) is seen throughout the Pacific, even off the coasts of Central and South America.

Of all the sea snakes, the beaked sea snake is generally considered most dangerous. It not only has an extremely toxic venom but also inhabits the shallow waters of beach areas where it may come in contact with people.

Miraculous cures for the bites of these snakes are sometimes reported in the Pacific area where they abound. Experts agree, however, that there is yet no really effective treatment for bites from sea snakes. It is fortunate that people are rarely bitten by these snakes.

**The banded sea snake
has a small head
and flat body and tail.**

ARE THESE THE FABLED SEA SERPENTS?

Sea snakes are not the sea serpents about which tales have been told since ancient times. First of all, the sea serpent stories originated in seas off Scandinavian countries—a part of the world where true sea snakes do not exist. And the true snakes are tiny as compared to the sea serpents of folk tales.

The mythical sea serpents were monsters said to have been sighted in the cold, icy waters, and while some stories persist to this day, it is generally agreed that no such creatures ever existed. Of course, people probably did see strange, unfamiliar creatures in the sea. Most of the hundreds of reports are cases of mistaken identity. A school of dolphins in a follow-the-leader procession, each animal rising periodically in arching leaps from the water, might very easily be mistaken for one huge and very long beast, particularly in misty, foggy weather. The tremendously long tentacles of a giant squid could also be mistaken for one or several big snakes writhing at the surface.

But real snakes to match the tales? They do not exist.

(5)
VIPERS

To many people any poisonous snake is a "viper." However, vipers really belong to a specific family (Viperidae) of poisonous snakes. The subfamily that lives in Europe, Asia, and Africa is often called true or Old World vipers to distinguish it from the other large subfamily, the pit vipers, which have a deep heat-sensitive pit between eye and nostril. There are no true vipers in the Americas where pit vipers are most abundant.

Many vipers are attractively colored. They have short tails and thick bodies, and, in most species, the head is broad and triangular. Vipers are sluggish snakes, usually slow or even reluctant to bite. There are exceptions, of course. Now and then an individual is easily irritated and is quick to bite. Vipers have huge, hollow fangs that fold back against the roof of the mouth when not in use. The snakes produce large quantities of venom. Vipers do not hunt actively for their prey as slim, swift snakes do. They wait for their meals to come close, then strike and kill their prey.

All the venomous snakes in Europe are vipers. The best known is the common viper, or adder. It is also the only poisonous snake found in Great Britain and Scandinavia. Because of its unusual tolerance to cold the common viper ranges north of the Arctic Circle—the only snake known to do so. In severe cold it hibernates, but sometimes it is active on sunny days when snow is still on the ground. The medical symbol, called the caduceus, shows two intertwined snakes that were probably modeled after the common European vipers. Today this snake is found mainly in mountains and forests. It is rarely more than 2 feet (.6 m) long.

The venom of the common viper is potent and can cause death, but it is rare for these snakes to bite unless they are picked up or stepped on. The amount of venom ejected is usually enough to kill the snake's prey, such as mice, shrews, and other small animals, in only a few minutes.

One of the most spectacular performances in nature is the dueling "dance" of two male common vipers. They push against each other with a fourth or more of their bodies lifted off the ground. Then, tightly pressed against each other, they weave back and forth. They do not attempt to bite and finally one of the two gives up. The victor apparently wins control over a particular territory and its females, but in actual mating it is not uncommon for one female to be attended by several males.

One of the common viper's relatives is Russell's viper of southern Asia. It is one of the most dangerous and feared of all poisonous snakes. The slow-moving 4- to 5-foot (1.2–1.5 m) snake hisses loudly when disturbed and strikes rapidly. The venom contains both hemotoxins like the venom of most rattlesnakes, and neurotoxins, like the venom of cobras and coral snakes. This makes the poison a double threat, and the bite is often fatal. Beause Russell's viper lives in areas where people regularly walk barefoot, the number of people bitten is high. Like other vipers, this snake gives birth to its young, often more than fifty at a time. The young are much more likely to strike than the parents.

Other well-known vipers include the African puff adder. If it is accidentally stepped on or grabbed, the puff adder strikes and bites, rarely making an effort to escape. During the day this broad-headed and grotesquely beautiful snake stays in hiding. At night it comes out to hunt rodents or other small animals, striking quickly to inject venom, then withdrawing and waiting until the victim dies. Often it uses its long fangs like hooks to help draw the kill into its mouth. Because of its abundance and wide distribution, the puff adder probably causes more deaths, than does any other poisonous snake of Africa. The African puff adder inflates its body and, like most vipers, hisses loudly when disturbed.

The smaller horned puff adder or sand viper is a light-colored desert dweller. It is distinguished by the prominent "horn" made of enlarged upturned scales over each eye. These serve as sand shields. The horned puff adder often hides in the sand. At the slightest disturbance it may strike from this hidden position.

The saw-scaled viper, another desert dweller, is easily excited, and its venom is especially toxic. Bites from snakes less than 1 foot (.3 m) long have been fatal to humans. If disturbed, the saw-scaled viper usually inflates its body and hisses as it expels air. It also makes a rasping noise by rubbing its rough scales together. This viper usually stays hidden in the sand during the day. If it is uncovered, it attacks quickly, and even small snakes may leap as much as a foot (.3 m) into the air.

The gaboon viper of Africa's tropical rain forest is the largest of the viper family. One of the most handsome of all

snakes, it is marked with gaudy patches of bright colors. This viper is enormously thick-bodied and slow, and possesses the largest fangs of any poisonous snake. The fangs of a 6-foot (1.8 m) gaboon viper may be 2 inches (5.1 cm) long. One snake may have enough venom in the tremendously swollen glands in its jaws to kill three or more people. But this monstrous snake, which averages more than 4 feet (1.2 m) in length, is not aggressive. It almost needs to be goaded before it will bite.

Skin and skull of a rhinoceros viper. The "horns" over its eyes protected them from sand.

(6)
PIT
VIPERS

Pit vipers are found most abundantly in the Americas. A few species live in Asia. They form a subfamily of the vipers and are distinguished by the deep pit or cavity on each side of the face between the eye and the nostril. This pit is a unique sensory organ that is highly sensitive to heat. With it the snakes can detect their warm-blooded prey at considerable distances, even in the dark.

RATTLESNAKES

The pit sensory organ is especially well developed in rattlesnakes. A rattlesnake does not have to explore the complete labyrinth of a rat's burrow, for example, or search every inch of a branch in a tree or bush for birds. This "heat detector" is especially useful for hunting at night when the difference is greatest between air temperature and the body temperature of the prey. The rattlesnake tracks its prey by scent, but the heat detectors, used for the final strike, enable rattlesnakes to hit their victims with deadly accuracy even in the dark.

**The dark spot between eye and nostril
is the heat-detecting sensory
pit of this rattlesnake.**

A rattlesnake strikes with amazing speed. Typically it first coils or draws its body into stiff loops. It strikes with roughly the front third of its body which it holds up S-shaped ready to make its attack.

Long fangs are located at the front of the rattlesnake's upper jaw. They are so long that when not in use they fold back and rest against the roof of the mouth. Next to each fang grow reserve fangs. These become functional when an old fang is lost or broken, which may happen two to four times a year. Like all vipers the rattlesnake has a very highly developed mechanism for injecting venom. The hollow fangs are like hypodermic needles. They are connected by a narrow tube or duct to huge poison glands, one on each side. When the snake strikes and sinks its fangs into a victim, jaw muscles contract to squeeze the venom into the wound. After striking, rattlesnakes do not hold on. Because of their long, needle-sharp fangs they do not have to chew to get their venom into the wound. They strike and remove their fangs immediately and then follow the victim until it dies. Then they swallow their meal whole, as all snakes do.

Rattlesnakes are well camouflaged. Their mottling of black and lighter colors make them difficult to see almost anywhere in the wild. A few years ago, for example, a forester went into a southern pine forest to mark some trees to be cleared by a crew to follow him in a few days. He used a broad brush to put whitewash marks on the tree trunks.

This western diamondback
is giving warning with
the rattles of its tail.
Note also the forked tongue.

The forester worked quickly, and the cutting crew was soon at work. Then one day they found and killed a huge diamondback rattlesnake that had a broad band of white paint across its back. Obviously it had been whitewashed by the forester, and he wonders to this day exactly where it was. The forester called it his "close brush with death."

Nature has also provided rattlesnakes with a rattle, a buzzing warning signal. But beware! The warning is not always used.

Typically, however, a molested or disturbed rattlesnake first coils and then vibrates its tail rapidly before striking. Vibrating the tail is not at all unusual among snakes. Many harmless snakes have this habit, and if the tail happens to strike dry leaves or twigs, the sound can be ominous. But rattlesnakes have a built-in buzzer. It consists of a number of dry "buttons," or hollow sections of skin at the tip of the tail. Depending on the size of the rattlesnake, the sound can be very loud or as soft as the buzzing of an insect.

Each time the rattlesnake sheds its skin, another of these dry buttons is added to the rattle. A healthy growing rattlesnake may shed several times every year, each time adding one more button. For this reason counting the buttons is not a reliable way to determine the rattlesnake's age. Each button does not, as is sometimes supposed, represent one year. Furthermore, some of the buttons may break off, particularly in older snakes.

The largest poisonous snake in North America is the eastern diamondback rattlesnake, which lives mainly in the coastal lowlands of the South. Most exceed a length of 3 feet (.9 m), and 9-foot (2.7 m) eastern diamondbacks have been reported. The fangs of a rattlesnake this large are more than 1 inch (2.5 cm). long. The body is incredibly heavy,

A rattlesnake sheds its skin
several times every year.

as thick through as a man's arm. The head is definitely wedge-shaped and clearly distinct from the neck. Young diamondbacks have a very visible diamond pattern on the back. Older snakes become darker, the diamond pattern growing obscure. This big and very powerful poisonous snake should unquestionably be avoided.

Its counterpart in the West is the slightly shorter western diamondback rattlesnake. It moves more quickly and seems to become irritated more easily than the eastern diamondback. In winter western diamondbacks regularly gather in large numbers in dens to hibernate. The very similar and really colorful red diamondback is found only on the scrubby hillsides of Baja and Southern California. Of the three, the red diamondback rattlesnake is generally the most active during the daytime. It is also the least aggressive.

Timber rattlesnakes, ranging from 3 to 6 feet (.9 to 1.8 m) in length, live in woods, brushy country, and rocky hillsides from Maine to Texas. Over this wide area they vary greatly in color and pattern. Basically the blotched body is gray, black, or yellowish brown. Those found in the southern coastal lowlands are called canebrake rattlers. In some areas the timber rattlesnake has dark bands on the body, and may be called the banded rattlesnake. In northern regions in winter large numbers of timber rattlesnakes—often many hundreds—assemble in the same rocky crevice to hibernate.

From the Great Plains westward, the western or prairie rattlesnake is most common. It averages about 3 feet (.9 m) in length and rarely grows to as much as 6 feet (1.8 m) long. This rattlesnake is active mainly in the daytime, and like the timber rattlesnake, it congregates in dens to hibernate in winter. The western rattlesnake is one of the most common in populated areas, and although it is not especially aggressive, it is responsible for a large share of the rattler bites in the United States.

Most unusual of the North American rattlers is the sidewinder. It lives in the deserts of the Southwest and like most desert dwellers, it stays out of the sun during the day by hiding in burrows or under rocks or debris. It comes out at night to feed. What makes the sidewinder unique is its way of moving—sideways. Crawling on a straight course through the sand is difficult, but the sidewinder has developed a method of moving rapidly. It throws a loop of its body out to the side, then quickly pulls the remainder of its body after this loop. This process is repeated again and again. The trail in the sand is a series of J-shaped marks. The direction of movement is at an oblique angle to the way the snake is facing. The sidewinder's eyes are protected from the sand by scales that form "horns" over each eye. Sidewinders are not large; few attain a length of 2 feet (.6 m). Their venom is potent, but because of the small size of the snake, it is not produced in great amounts.

The massasauga in the Midwest and the pygmy rattlesnake of the southeastern United States are small, rarely as much as 2½ feet (.8 m). These little rattlesnakes have nine oversized scales on top of the head. For this reason they are called "mailed" rattlesnakes. Their rattles are small, making only an insectlike buzzing noise. Both have bad tempers and are quick to bite if disturbed. Deaths from their bites are rare, however, because they do not have large amounts of venom.

More than half a dozen other species of rattlesnakes, most with limited ranges, live in North America, and there are more members of the rattlesnake family in Mexico and in

**Left: sidewinder rattlesnake. Note the
protective shield over the eye. Above:
Eastern diamondback rattlesnake—the
largest poisonous snake in North America.**

Central and South America. The Mexican diamond rattle-snake, for example, often reaches a length of 5 feet (1.5 m), and like the diamondback rattlesnakes it produces lots of venom.

The cascabel, or tropical rattlesnake, of Central and South America, is another rattlesnake that often reaches a length of 5 feet (1.5 m) and is sometimes longer. The cascabel is the most dangerous species of rattlesnake, and it is a major cause of death due to snakebite in South America. The venom of the cascabel is different from that of North American rattlers. The North American rattlers have venom that is mostly hemotoxic, affecting the blood vessels and the area surrounding the bite. The venom of the cascabel has a much greater effect on the nervous system. Unusual, too, is the fact that the cascabel's venom seems to relax the neck muscles. A bite victim has difficulty holding up his head. The cascabel is thus said to "break the neck" of the people it bites.

OTHER
PIT VIPERS

In addition to the fifteen species of rattlesnakes two other pit vipers live in the United States. These are the copperhead and the cottonmouth, or water moccasin.

Copperheads inhabit almost every kind of country, from rocky hillsides to dry woodlands. They are found throughout the South from Florida to Texas and on the east coast as far north as Massachusetts. These attractive snakes have brownish red "hourglass" patterns on a lighter background. The top of the head is shiny and coppery.

Copperheads are the most common poisonous snakes in the eastern United States. Fortunately they are not quick to bite. Most bites occur when someone steps on a snake. Climbers or berry pickers may put a hand too close to a sunning or resting snake. The bites are extremely painful. The area around the wound swells up immediately. But the venom is mild and rarely causes death.

Few copperheads are more than 3 feet (.9 m) long, but occasional individuals reach a length of 4½ feet (1.4 m) or more. Like other pit vipers the copperhead has a thick body, a distinctly triangular head, and vertical pupils in its eyes. The copperhead also has a habit of vibrating its tail like a rattlesnake when disturbed. It does not have a rattle, but if the tail hits dried leaves, the noise is much the same. Like nearly all other pit vipers the copperhead gives birth to its young, usually fewer than a dozen. The tip of a young snake's tail is yellow. The tail is lifted and waved, probably to hold the attention of prey while the snake moves close enough for the deadly bite.

The cottonmouth, or water moccasin, is a close relative of the copperhead, but it lives in lowlands, swampy areas, and along streams throughout the Southeast. Young cotton-mouths have a distinct dark pattern on a lighter brown background, and the tip of the tail, like that of young copper-heads, is bright yellow. Older snakes become dark all over and grow very heavy, with a big, broad head. A disturbed snake may gape repeatedly to display the cottony white interior of its mouth before it actually strikes. This very dangerous snake basks along the shore, and if come upon suddenly, it is more like to coil ready to strike than to try to escape.

The copperhead and cottonmouth have close relatives in other countries. One is the cantil that lives in the swampy lowlands of Mexico and Central America. It is a satiny dark-brown snake with two light-yellow stripes on each side of its head. Other dangerous relatives are the sharp-nosed pit viper of southern China and the mamushi of Japan.

Among the most unusual of these poisonous snakes are the more than two dozen species of lancehead pit vipers of southeastern Asia and nearby islands. All have an exceptionally broad, flat head that is clearly set off from the narrow neck, much like the head of a spear. The large species, some of them more than 5 feet (1.5 m) long, are highly dangerous because of the great amount of venom they produce. Smaller species give painful bites but rarely cause death. On one island off Malaya, the snakes are worshiped in a special temple where many of them are kept and allowed to roam freely.

The largest, most famous, and most fearsome of the lancehead pit vipers live in South America. Of the several dozen species the best known is the *fer-de-lance* that lives on the island of Martinique. A closely related species is found on St. Lucia Island. The snake's French name of *fer-de-lance* (literally "lance-iron" or "spearhead") refers to the shape of its big head. A similar pit viper goes by the Spanish name *barba amarilla* ("yellow beard"), referring to its bright yellow chin. It lives in the tropical forests of Mexico and of Central and South America.

The bushmaster is the largest poisonous snake in the New World.

These big snakes grow to more than 7 feet (2.1 m) long. They eat mainly rats and mice. Hunting for these rodents takes the snakes into fields and also into houses and other buildings, and as a result, they often come in contact with humans. Their bites are often fatal. They cause more deaths in the Americas than do any other poisonous snakes.

The bushmaster, a pit viper found in remote mountainous jungles of Central and South America, is the largest poisonous snake in the New World. In fact, throughout the world, only the king cobra is larger among poisonous snakes. The bushmaster may reach a length of 12 feet (3.7 m).

Slender and pinkish, with blotches of black and brown, the bushmaster has excellent camouflage as it moves or rests in the leaves of the forest floor where it lives. The female bushmaster lays eggs, usually about a dozen, and then coils around them until they hatch. Her presence probably contributes little to incubating the eggs, but she may defend them from intruders.

In some countries the bushmaster goes by the name of *cascabela muda*, which means "silent rattler." The bushmaster is far from silent, however. Though it does not have a rattle, the tail ends in a peculiar spiny burr. When an irritated snake vibrates its tail rapidly, this hard tip makes a very loud noise if it strikes leaves, sticks, or any other objects. A bushmaster also has long fangs—sometimes more than 1 inch (2.5 cm) long—and produces great amounts of venom. Fortunately for people, bushmasters are not common.

(7)
WHERE POISONOUS SNAKES LIVE

Poisonous snakes exist almost everywhere in the world. The common European viper even ranges north of the Arctic Circle.

Of the heavily populated regions of the world, Europe has the fewest poisonous snakes. The continent is too cool for most snakes, and over the centuries, habitats have been destroyed, and snakes have been killed off with the development of agriculture and industry. All of the poisonous snakes in Europe belong to the viper family, and only the Levantine viper is really very dangerous. It lives on some of the islands in the Mediterranean.

Snakes are uncommon also in the hot, dry deserts of Africa. Two kinds of cobras live in the area. One is the famous asp, or Egyptian cobra. The African garter snake and the desert black snake, members of the same family as cobras, also live here, but true vipers are the most abundant of the poisonous snakes in North Africa. Among them are the African horned viper, the saw-scaled viper, several species of mole vipers, and the African puff adder.

South of the big desert region in Africa the number of

poisonous snakes increases. Among the familiar and dangerous species are four kinds of mambas, six kinds of cobras, the gaboon viper, the puff adder, and a number of other vipers. Here also are the boomslang and the bird snake, the two poisonous snakes of the colubrid family. The poisonous snakes in this part of the world total nearly thirty species. There are not many people where these snakes live, and so the number of deaths caused by snakebite is relatively low.

There are no poisonous snakes (or snakes of any kind) on Madagascar off Africa's southeastern coast. Geographic isolation has spared the island.

Northwestern Asia and the Middle East are mainly desert, and few snakes live there. Among them are two kinds of cobras, the desert black snake, several species of mole vipers, the horned viper, the saw-scaled viper, several kinds of adders, and three species of pit vipers.

Poisonous snakes are abundant in Southeast Asia. Over many centuries they have become adapted to a life close to centers of population. Among these snakes are about twelve species of coral snakes, two species of cobras, including the king cobra (the giant of all poisonous snakes), about six species of vipers, and some forty species of pit vipers. Many of these snakes range northward into China, and some live on nearby islands.

Of all areas in the world Australia and the nearby Pacific islands have the most unusual population of snakes. About 60 percent of the species in Australia are poisonous, and so are about 25 percent of the species of snakes of New Guinea. Many of these poisonous snakes are small, and their venom is mild. But the venom of others is powerful, and several species are ranked among the most dangerous in the world.

A palm viper—widespread in South America.

All of the poisonous snakes of the Australia–New Guinea area belong to the same family (Elapidae) as cobras. Most of them look harmless, resembling North American racers and king snakes. All are ground dwellers, only a few kinds venturing even into low bushes. Of the many kinds the most dangerous are the taipan, the tiger snake, the death adder, the black snake, and the brown snake. In the waters around Australia are the even more poisonous but mild-tempered sea snakes.

South America's poisonous snakes are most abundant in the tropics. Some of the species range northward into Central America and Mexico. Among them are more than forty species of coral snakes, and forty species of lancehead pit vipers (of which the *barba amarilla* is best known), two species of rattlesnakes, and the rare and dangerous bushmaster.

In North America there are nineteen species of poisonous snakes. These include two species of coral snakes, fifteen species of rattlesnakes, the copperhead, and the cottonmouth. There are no poisonous snakes in Alaska and only a few in Canada where they are found only in the southern provinces.

(8)
WHAT TO DO ABOUT SNAKEBITE

"Prevention is the best cure" applies above all to snakebite. Don't try to catch, kill, or handle a poisonous snake. About one-third of the snake bites in the United States are received this way. And most bites occur close to home, not on camping or hiking trips. In areas where poisonous snakes live, children playing in woods or fields may be bitten. Or people reaching for a log in a woodpile or doing chores out of doors may accidentally startle and alarm a snake.

But most snakes, including those that pack poison, are not at all anxious to fight. If you are a snake's length away from a snake, you are probably perfectly safe. Poisonous snakes—particularly those of the New World—will not come after you or chase you.

If you are hiking or camping where there are habitats for poisonous snakes, just take sensible precautions. Wear boots or high-topped shoes with trousers over them. Watch where you step, reach, or sit. Don't put your hands under rocks or logs, or into places where you cannot see. Be careful when climbing steep slopes or cliffs where snakes like to bask in the sun. Check before you step over a log; a snake might be

lying on the other side. Step onto the log first and look on the other side. Be careful in caves, particularly near the entrances. Snakes generally avoid bright daylight, and in cool weather large numbers commonly assemble in caves or in rocky crevices to hibernate. Don't crawl under fences or low brush unless you can see clearly that there are no snakes.

Even if you think a snake is dead, don't pick it up. Snakes have remarkable reflex actions—a snake that seems dead may suddenly "spring to life."

But accidents can happen. In case of snakebite what should you do? First, get medical help as soon as possible —even if there is no immediate pain or other reaction. Second, keep the victim calm and quiet. Do not let the victim run. Frantic emotion and activity only help to pump the venom through the system.

You may try to suck the venom out of the wound if you have no open cuts in your mouth. But don't make cuts or slashes across the bite.

Not long ago common treatment for snakebite was to apply a tourniquet, slash the bite area, and suck the wound. Nowadays we know that, except for suction this is not a good treatment—especially by someone without professional experience. The bites of many snakes (vipers for instance) may be made worse by the use of a tourniquet. The tourniquet first pools the venom destructively around the bite area, and then when released "dumps" the venom into the system with

The rock ledge is a typical hiding place for snakes like this copperhead.

harmful results. Cutting is unnecessary and extremely dangerous if the bite is near an artery. Antivenin, too, should only be given by a doctor or an experienced person who understands how to treat possible reactions to it.

People throughout history have had emotional and fearful reactions to snakes. Merely discussing snakebite may make a reader feel as if there were "killer snakes" lying in wait behind every bush. This is simply not true.

Remember, if you give them a chance, snakes will flee rather than attack. In the United States deaths from snakebite are extremely rare, and professional medical attention could prevent the few that do occur.

(9)
WHERE TO FIND MORE INFORMATION

In areas where there are poisonous snakes, you can get information locally that tells you how to identify them and what to do if you are bitten. You can learn also about first aid for bites and the sources for medical aid and antivenins.

Many books about snakes are available. Libraries may have good books that are out of print and not available in bookstores. Be sure to look among the juvenile and adult books to find those of special interest.

Arnold, R. E. *What to Do About Bites and Stings of Venomous Animals.* New York: Collier Books, 1973.

Behler, J. L. and King, F. W., *The Audubon Society Field Guide to North American Reptiles and Amphibians.* New York: Alfred A. Knopf, 1979.

Cochran, Doris M. and Coleman, J. Goin. *The New Field Book of Reptiles and Amphibians.* New York: Putnam's, 1970.

Curran, C. H. and Kauffeld, Carl. *Snakes and Their Ways.* New York: Harper and Brothers, 1937.

Ditmars, Raymond L. *Snakes of the World.* New York: Macmillan, 1966.

Harrison, Hal H. *The World of the Snake.* Phila. and New York: Lippincott, 1971.

Kinghorn, J. R. *The Snakes of Australia.* Sydney: Angus and Robertson, 1956.

Minton, S. A., Jr. and Minton, M. G. *Venomous Reptiles.* New York: Charles Scribner's Sons, 1969.

Oliver, James A. *Snakes in Fact and Fiction.* New York: Macmillan, 1958.

Parrish, Henry M. *Poisonous Snakebites in the United States.* New York: Vantage Press, 1971.

Pinney, Roy. *The Snake Book.* New York: Doubleday & Company, Inc., 1981.

Pope, Clifford H. *The Giant Snakes.* New York: Alfred A. Knopf, 1975.

        The Poisonous Snakes of the New World. N.Y. Zoological Society, 1944.

        The Reptile World. New York: Alfred A. Knopf, 1974.

Rose, Walter. *Snakes—Mainly South African.* Capetown; Maskew Limited, 1955.

Russell, Findlay E. *Snake Venom Poisoning.* New York: J. B. Lippincott, 1980.

Schmidt, Karl P. and Inger, Robert F. *Living Reptiles of the World.* New York Hanover House, 1957.

Simon, Hilda. *Easy Identification Guide to North American Snakes.* New York: Dodd, Mead, 1979.

Stidworthy, John. *Snakes of the World.* New York: Paul Hamlyn, 1969.

Stonehouse, Bernard. *A Closer Look at Reptiles.* New York; Franklin Watts, 1979.

INDEX